# Disciple**Way**

*7 Disciplines for Maturing in Christ*

# Serving

*Project Directors:* Philip Attebery, D.Min., Steve Crawley
*Writers:* John Adams, D.Min., Danny Pitts, Judy Wallace, Todd West
*Content Managers:* Philip Attebery, D.Min., Chris George, Ronnie Johnson, Ph.D., Jake Vandenburg
*Editor:* Jerome Cooper
*Design Team:* Ken Adams, Julie Parker, Larry Thompson

DiscipleWay Serving
ISBN 978-0-89114-478-1

# DiscipleWay Serving

**Contents**

# 6.0 Serving

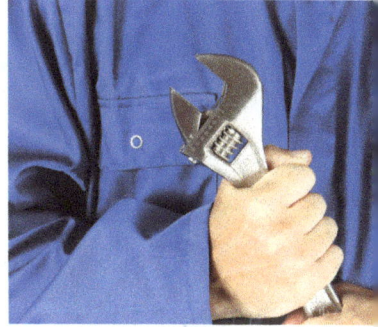

A true disciple does not just sit around and do nothing. Christians are supposed to serve. Serving is the action of doing something for someone other than yourself. Upon completion of this series of lessons, you will understand serving, be inspired to serve God and others, and be able to serve. You should also be able to lead others in the discipline of service. The principle of serving is easily understood but hard to practice. Serving is a discipline every Christian should practice. The rewards of service outweigh the struggle. Immediate rewards of service include a closer relationship with Jesus, a clear conscience, seeing souls saved, and many others. The costs of discipleship are indeed high — at times they have included rejection, shame, and death. Individual Christians are also gifted to serve their local church. Christians should know and use their gift.

- The disciple will grow to understand the biblical basis for service.

- The disciple will grow in the desire to serve God and others.

- The disciple will be able to serve and lead others to serve.

**Carry-Through Activity.** Create a service project or projects to be performed.

# Serving Defined

## Destination

Service to the Lord is a vital part of maturing as a Christian and becoming a true disciple of Christ. It is best that we find our definition of service or being a servant directly from the Bible.

**Lesson Aim:** The disciple is able to give a biblical explanation of serving.

---

### Disciple**Words**

*Passage: Deuteronomy 6:13; Matthew 4:8-11; Galatians 5:13-14*

*Key Verse: Deuteronomy 6:13*

---

**Preparation for the trip checklist:**

- ◯ I have prayed faithfully for myself and m[y] disciple(s) and/or disciple maker.
- ◯ I have read the lesson aim.
- ◯ I have read and studied the Bible passage[.]
- ◯ I have memorized the key verse.
- ◯ I have completed my personal disciplesh[ip] assignments and am prepared to evaluate/be evaluated by my fellow disciples.

What is your definition of *service?*

Who taught you how to serve?

Temptation often comes after spiritual growth or victory. Jesus faced temptation after His baptism. By practicing the spiritual disciplines you have studied so far, you may need to be extra diligent in guarding your heart from Satan's similar temptations.

Study the Bible passages to forge the truths into principles. Pray for God's instruction in finding the principles to apply. Study the passages, answering the three basic inductive Bible study questions.

Read Matthew 4:8-11.

## Observation

1. Who is the author?

2. Who is involved/addressed?

3. When was the book written? When does it take place?

4. What are the key words? (nouns, verbs)

5. What key words/phrases are repeated?

6. What is being compared? (like, as)

7. What is being contrasted? (but)

8. What are the cause/effect relationships? (therefore, for)

9. What form is used? (parable, narrative, poetry)

# Interpretation

1. How is the passage affected by its biblical/historical context?

2. How does the passage relate to its immediate context?

3. How does this passage compare with other related passages?

4. What terms or ideas need to be researched?

5. Summarize the passage/paragraph in one sentence (main idea).

# Application

1. Is there a promise to claim or a truth to believe?

2. Is there an example to follow?

3. Is there an attitude to change or a sin to confess?

4. Is there a command to obey?

5. Is there an error to avoid?

6. Is there something to praise God for?

Read together Galatians 5:13-14. Follow the steps of the inductive method you have learned.

- Observation — What does the passage say?




- Interpretation — What does the passage mean?




- Application — How does the passage apply?

**1. Define service:**

**2. Discussion.** Discuss specific questions about your own service.

- How are you serving God?
- How are you serving others?
- How are you serving your community?

**3. Pray Through Scripture.** Using experience gained from the *DiscipleWay* lessons on prayer, pray through Matthew 4:9-11.

**4. Carry-Through Activity.** Begin (or enhance) a service project. Begin the project by researching areas of potential service. Consult your pastor for ideas. Is there a ministry or lay ministry in the church that needs workers? Are there shut-ins or elderly in your church who perhaps can use help in home cleaning or auto maintenance? If not there are usually many avenues of service available. (For example, contact a local nursing home and inquire about opportunities such as leading a Bible study, worship services, or craft activity. If you live in a college town, adopt a student whose family is far away. Offer to do laundry, prepare home-cooked meals, and friendship.)

**5. Service Project.** Use the following guide to fill out, pray about, discuss, and decide together on a carry-through service project.

- What are your talents?
- What are your spiritual gifts?
- What opportunities are available in your church?
- What opportunities are available in your city?
- What time can you do the service?
- Will there be any cost involved?
- Can any service be done anonymously?

## Evaluation

What is your definition of service now? Has your definition changed?

What have you learned about your own ability to serve?

How has this study helped you serve?

In what areas are you presently serving God and others?

### Get ready for the next session

Continue researching your service project and be ready to decide on one next week. Conduct inductive Bible study of the following passage before the next session: John 13:1-35. Read Mark 10:43-45 and Philippians 2:1-8.

# Motivated for Serving

**Destination**

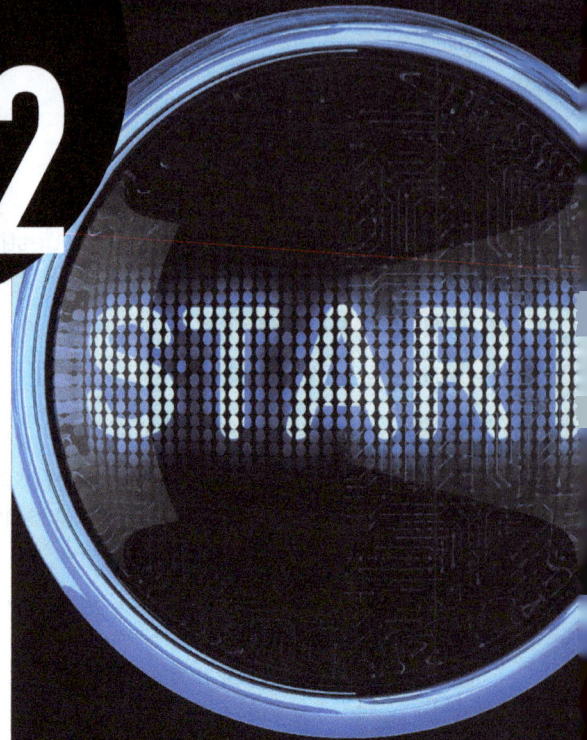

*Motivation* is defined as "the act of giving somebody a reason to do something." What motivates you to serve? Two main types of motivation are commonly recognized. External motivation comes from outside the person while internal motivation comes from within a person. Examples of external motivation are rewards, avoidance of punishment, and approval of others, whereas examples of internal motivation include responsibility, guilt, and emotions. There is another, more powerful eternal motivation, which comes from God.

**Lesson Aim:** The disciple is to examine his/her motivation for serving.

---

**Disciple**Words
*Passage: John 13:1-35*
*Key Verse: Philippians 2:5*

---

**Preparation for the trip checklist:**
- ❍ I have prayed faithfully for myself and disciple(s) and/or disciple maker.
- ❍ I have read the lesson aim.
- ❍ I have read and studied the Bible passa
- ❍ I have memorized the key verse.
- ❍ I have completed my personal disciple assignments and am prepared to evalu be evaluated by my fellow disciples.
- ❍ I have prepared for the "act of kindne that I will perform during this session

Foot-washing was a cultural phenomenon during the time of Christ. Consider performing a similar task for each other (shine shoes, do laundry, etc.).

Read John 13. What is the setting of this chapter?

Who was with Jesus at the time?

What did Jesus do in this passage?

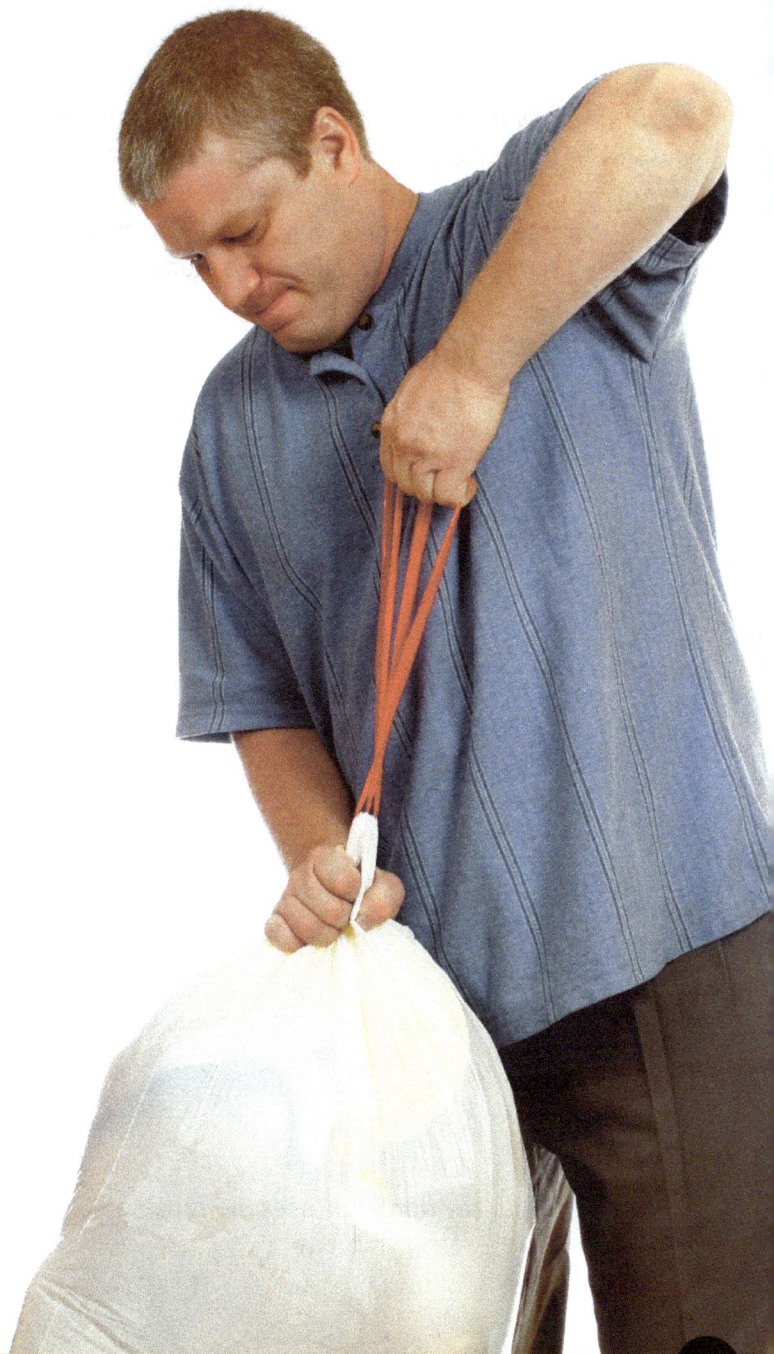

Study the Bible passages to forge the truths into principles. Pray for God's instruction in finding the principles to apply. Study the passages, beginning with John 13, answering the three basic inductive Bible study questions.

# Observation

1. Who is the author?

2. Who is involved/addressed?

3. When was the book written? When does it take place?

4. What are the key words? (nouns, verbs)

5. What key words/phrases are repeated?

6. What is being compared? (like, as)

7. What is being contrasted? (but)

8. What are the cause/effect relationships? (therefore, for)

9. What form is used? (parable, narrative, poetry)

# Interpretation

1. How is the passage affected by its biblical/historical context?

2. How does the passage relate to its immediate context?

3. How does this passage compare with other related passages?

4. What terms or ideas need to be researched?

5. Summarize the passage/paragraph in one sentence (main idea).

# Application

1. Is there a promise to claim or a truth to believe?

2. Is there an example to follow?

3. Is there an attitude to change or a sin to confess?

4. Is there a command to obey?

5. Is there an error to avoid?

6. Is there something to praise God for?

Compare verse 1 with verse 35. What is the common theme? Love is the motivation for service!

How does your pre-lesson study of Mark 10:43-45 relate to this study? Apply the inductive method to this passage.

- Observation — what does the passage say?

- Interpretation — what does the passage mean?

- Application — how does the passage apply?

How does your pre-lesson study of Philippians 2:1-8 relate to this passage? Apply the inductive method to this passage.

- Observation — what does the passage say?

- Interpretation — what does the passage mean?

- Application — how does the passage apply?

**1. Explore your motivation for service.** Is your motivation external? Is there someone or something outside yourself (such as what others think about you, attempting to impress God, etc.) that makes you want to serve?

Is your motivation internal? Is there an internal motivation (such as pride, competition, or guilt) that makes you want to serve?

Is your motivation eternal? Is there lasting motivation? (such as God's Word, Jesus' example, and the leading of the Holy Spirit) that makes you want to serve?

**2. What if no one notices your service?** Foot-washing was a cultural phenomenon. Consider performing a small task for someone else. Take a break and perform a "random act of kindness." Come back together and discuss the results. (For example, clean all windshields in the parking lot, clean house if meeting in a home, etc.)

What was your attitude as you performed this task? Did anyone see you?

Do you want others to see or know you do them?

How do you feel about serving in secret?

How do you incorporate previous disciplines into service?

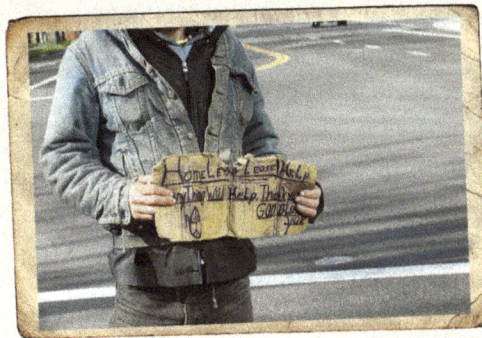

Is service an act of worship?

**3. Pray Through Scripture** — Philippians 2:1-8. How do we follow the example Jesus set for us? Motivation for service includes gratitude for the great things God has done for us. What great things has God done for you? List them.

**4. Carry-Through Activity.** Select your service project. Plan to do the project during the next session. Either meet at the specific place of service or reserve time to go there together after the Bible study portion of the next session.

## Evaluation

How do you have the "same mind" that Jesus has for serving?

What is your motivation for serving? Some focus on works as a means of grace (i.e., the way to get to heaven, receive eternal life).

However many others focus on works as a means of recognition and outward acceptance. Winning souls is not a contest. It is a way of showing concern for the lost. God is not impressed by how many scriptures you have memorized. While scripture memorization is good, God looks to see if the scripture truth has been internalized in your heart. Because one church has a higher attendance than another does not mean that it is better or more scriptural. Even good deeds can be done with wrong motives. Do you live to impress human beings, or to serve God? Just because you act like a disciple, does not mean that your heart is right. When God looks on your heart, what does He see?

### Get ready for the next session

Make any arrangements necessary to begin your service project. This includes planning to meet at the location for lesson 6.3, or to go there immediately following 6.3 Bible study. Conduct inductive Bible study of the following passage before the next session: John 15:1-8.

# Power to Serve

**Destination**

Where do you get the power to serve? Power is the ability, strength, and capacity to do something. If you try to serve God and others in your own power, you will face stress, exhaustion, burnout, or even failure. The ultimate goal is a life lived in ministering to the needs of others through the power of the Holy Spirit for the glory of God.

**Lesson Aim:** The disciple will understand that power to serve comes from Jesus.

DiscipleWords
*Passage: John 15:1-8*
*Key Verse: John 15:5*

**Preparation for the trip checklist:**
- ○ I have prayed faithfully for myself and my disciple(s) and/or disciple maker.
- ○ I have read the lesson aim.
- ○ I have read and studied the Bible passage.
- ○ I have memorized the key verse.
- ○ I have completed my personal discipleship assignments and am prepared to evaluate/be evaluated by my fellow disciples.
- ○ I have made the necessary preparations for the service project to be performed during this session.

Review session 6.2. You are meeting at the location of service project or have made plans to go directly after the Bible study portion of this lesson.

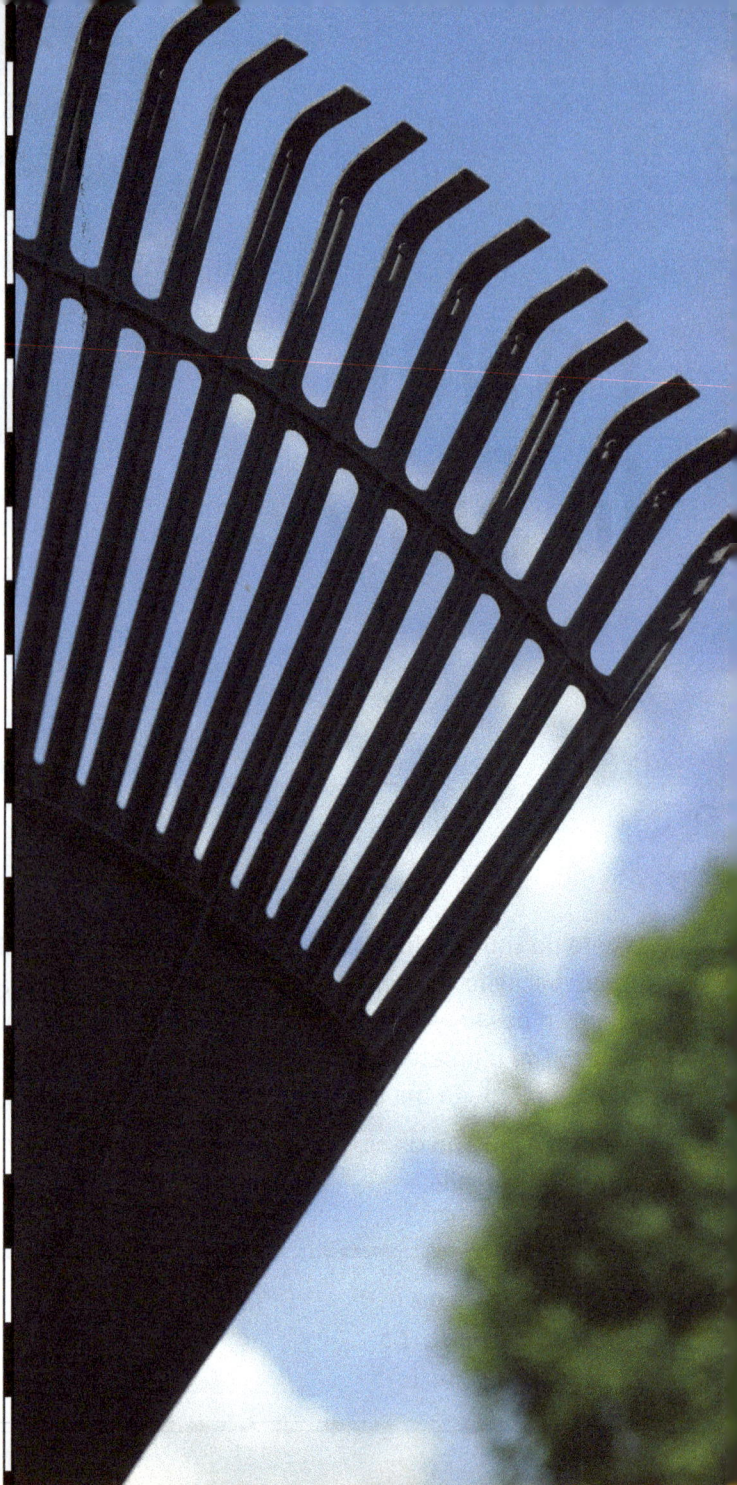

Study John 15:1-8 to forge the truths into principles. Pray for God's instruction in finding the principles to apply. Study the passages, answering the three basic inductive Bible study questions.

# Observation

1. Who is the author?

2. Who is involved/addressed?

3. When was the book written? When does it take place?

4. What are the key words? (nouns, verbs)

5. What key words/phrases are repeated?

6. What is being compared? (like, as)

7. What is being contrasted? (but)

8. What are the cause/effect relationships? (therefore, for)

9. What form is used? (parable, narrative, poetry)

# Interpretation

1. How is the passage affected by its biblical/historical context?

2. What is the immediate context? How does the passage relate to its immediate context?

3. How does this passage compare with other related passages?

4. What terms or ideas need to be researched?

5. Summarize the passage/paragraph in one sentence (main idea).

## Application

1. Is there a promise to claim or a truth to believe?

2. Is there an example to follow?

3. Is there an attitude to change or a sin to confess?

4. Is there a command to obey?

5. Is there an error to avoid?

6. Is there something to praise God for?

**1. Explore the degree to which you abide in Christ versus depending on yourself.**

**2. Pray Through Scripture.** Pray through John 15:1-8.

**3. Carry-Through Activity — The Service Project.** Begin working on your service project. Spend about an hour in service, depending on the kind of project selected.

**4. Discussion.** Debrief and discuss with your group afterward.

- What you did

- Your feelings about your service

- Your motivation to serve

- The degree to which you abide in Jesus for power to serve.

## Evaluation

How much do you abide in Jesus to bear fruit?

### Get ready for the next session

Make any arrangements necessary to continue your service project.

Conduct inductive Bible study of the following passage before the next session: John 15:9-17.

# Abide in Love

Sometimes simply getting started is the most difficult part of a task. The same is true in the area of service for a Christian. Many do nothing because they do not feel they are qualified. Some are ready to jump to it but don't know exactly how or where to start. Still others tend to think that service is applicable to only certain Christians called into full-time ministry. As Jesus gave His final instructions to His disciples before His death, He emphasized how our love for Him is displayed in our obedience to come alongside other people and love them to the point of setting aside our lives for theirs. Although the *laying aside* is death, it can also refer to giving up our dreams, desires, wishes, plans, goals, and visions to help one another. It can even be as seemingly small as giving up some time or our own planned daily agenda to be available to serve others for the Lord.

**Lesson Aim:** The disciple serves because of love.

**Destination**

---

Disciple**Words**

*Passage: John 15:9-17*
*Key Verse: John 15:9*

---

**Preparation for the trip checklist:**
- ○ I have prayed faithfully for myself and my disciple(s) and/or disciple maker.
- ○ I have read the lesson aim.
- ○ I have read and studied the Bible passage.
- ○ I have memorized the key verse.
- ○ I have completed my personal disciplesh[i] assignments and am prepared to evaluate be evaluated by my fellow disciples.
- ○ I have made the necessary preparations for the service project for this session.

Review session 6.3. If you did not have the opportunity during the last session, discuss your actions, feelings, and results of the service you performed. For this session you are meeting at the location of service project or have made plans to go directly after the Bible study portion of this lesson.

Study John 15:9-17 to forge the truths into principles. Pray for God's instruction in finding the principles to apply. Answer the three basic inductive Bible study questions.

# Observation

1. Who is the author?

2. Who is involved/addressed?

3. When was the book written? When does it take place?

4. What are the key words? (nouns, verbs)

5. What key words/phrases are repeated?

6. What is being compared? (like, as)

7. What is being contrasted? (but)

8. What are the cause/effect relationships? (therefore, for)

9. What form is used? (parable, narrative, poetry)

# Interpretation

1. How is the passage affected by its biblical/ historical context?

2. How does the passage relate to its immediate context?

3. How does this passage compare with other related passages?

4. What terms or ideas need to be researched?

5. Summarize the passage/paragraph in one sentence (main idea).

## Application

1. Is there a promise to claim or a truth to believe?

2. Is there an example to follow?

3. Is there an attitude to change or a sin to confess?

4. Is there a command to obey?

5. Is there an error to avoid?

6. Is there something to praise God for?

**1. Discussion.** Discuss ways love can help you avoid exhaustion. Do you ever get tired of serving? How do you show love to unlovable people?

**2. Pray Through Scripture** — Pray through John 15:9-17.

**3. Carry-Through Activity — The Service Project.** Continue working on your service project. Spend about an hour depending on the kind of project selected.

**4. Debrief.** Debrief and discuss with your group afterward.

● What you did.

● Your feelings about your service.

● The commandment of Jesus to love one another.

## Evaluation

Are you motivated by Jesus' example of and commandment to love?

### Get ready for the next session

Make any arrangements necessary to continue your service project. Conduct inductive Bible study of the following passage before the next session: John 15:18-27.

# Hated for Serving

One of the most difficult things that a servant of God faces is criticism. This can come in the form of being misunderstood, unappreciated, or by direct persecution. In this lesson we will help the disciple develop a plan of action for dealing with the critics he or she may encounter at home, work, school, or even church.

**Lesson Aim:** The disciple can expect persecution for serving God.

DiscipleWords
*Passage: John 15:18-27*
*Key Verse: John 15:19*

**Preparation for the trip checklist:**
❍ I have prayed faithfully for myself and my disciple(s) and/or disciple maker.
❍ I have read the lesson aim.
❍ I have read and studied the Bible passage.
❍ I have memorized the key verse.
❍ I have completed my personal discipleship assignments and am prepared to evaluate/be evaluated by my fellow disciples.
❍ I have made the necessary preparations for the service project for this session.

Destination

Review session 6.4. If you did not have the opportunity last week, discuss your actions, feelings, and results of the service you performed. This week you are meeting at the location of service project or have made plans to go directly after the Bible study portion of this lesson.

What do you consider your natural gifts and spiritual gifts to be? How can you use those gifts in the church and in the community?

Study John 15:18-27 to forge the truths into principles. Pray for God's instruction in finding the principles to apply. Study the passages, answering the three basic inductive Bible study questions.

## Observation

1. Who is the author?

2. Who is involved/addressed?

3. When was the book written? When does it take place?

4. What are the key words? (nouns, verbs)

5. What key words/phrases are repeated?

6. What is being compared? (like, as)

7. What is being contrasted? (but)

8. What are the cause/effect relationships? (therefore, for)

9. What form is used? (parable, narrative, poetry)

## Interpretation

1. How is the passage affected by its biblical/historical context?

2. How does the passage relate to its immediate context?

3. How does this passage compare with other related passages?

4. What terms or ideas need to be researched?

5. Summarize the passage/paragraph in one sentence (main idea).

## Application

1. Is there a promise to claim or a truth to believe?

2. Is there an example to follow?

3. Is there an attitude to change or a sin to confess?

4. Is there a command to obey?

5. Is there an error to avoid?

6. Is there something to praise God for?

**1. Discussion.** Discuss ways criticism may discourage you from service (make you less likely to serve). Have you been criticized or faced opposition during your current service? What is the harshest form of hatred Christians face? What is the mildest form of hatred Christians face?

**2. Pray Through Scripture.** Pray through John 15:18-27.

**3. Carry-Through Activity — The Service Project.** Continue working on your service project. Spend about an hour depending on the kind of project selected.

**4. Debrief.** Debrief and discuss with your group afterward.

- What you did

- Your feelings about your service

- The commandment of Jesus to love one another

## Evaluation

What will you do when you face hatred?

### Get ready for the next session

Make any arrangements necessary to continue your service project. Conduct inductive Bible study of the following passage before the next session: Romans 12:1-8.

Your leader will provide you with a spiritual gifts inventory. Complete the survey before your next session.

# Gifted to Serve

Destination

We are born with certain inborn traits. Some of those are physical and some of those have to do with our personalities. When we are *born again*, God gives us spiritual gifts that enable us to contribute to the church. You have at least one. Spiritual gifts are the abilities given and empowered by the Holy Spirit.

**Lesson Aim:** The disciple understands the purpose of spiritual gifts.

Disciple**Words**
*Passage: Romans 12:1-8*
*Key Verse: Romans 12:3*

**Preparation for the trip checklist:**
- ❍ I have prayed faithfully for myself and m[y] disciple(s) and/or disciple maker.
- ❍ I have read the lesson aim.
- ❍ I have read and studied the Bible passage
- ❍ I have memorized the key verse.
- ❍ I have completed my personal disciplesh[ip] assignments and am prepared to evaluate/be evaluated by my fellow disciples.
- ❍ I have made the necessary preparations for the service project for this session.

Review session 6.5. If you did not have the opportunity during the last session, discuss your actions, feelings, and results of the service you performed. This week you are meeting at the location of service project or have made plans to go directly after the Bible study portion of this lesson.

Read the Bible passages aloud together. The apostle Paul described the purpose and nature of spiritual gifts in letters to believers in churches he had started. The first of these is the letter to the Romans. Read the passage together.

Study Romans 12:1-8 to forge the truths into principles. Pray for God's instruction in finding the principles to apply. Study the passage, answering the three basic inductive Bible study questions.

# Observation

1. Who is the author?

2. Who is involved/addressed?

3. When was the book written? When does it take place?

4. What are the key words? (nouns, verbs)

5. What key words/phrases are repeated?

6. What is being compared? (like, as)

7. What is being contrasted? (but)

8. What are the cause/effect relationships? (therefore, for)

9. What form is used? (parable, narrative, poetry)

# Interpretation

1. How is the passage affected by its biblical/historical context?

2. How does the passage relate to its immediate context?

3. How does this passage compare with other related passages?

4. What terms or ideas need to be researched?

5. Summarize the passage/paragraph in one sentence (main idea).

## Application

1. Is there a promise to claim or a truth to believe?

2. Is there an example to follow?

3. Is there an attitude to change or a sin to confess?

4. Is there a command to obey?

5. Is there an error to avoid?

6. Is there something to praise God for?

**1. Three main passages in the Bible mention spiritual gifts.** Do you know where the other two are? Find them and prepare a list of all gifts listed in the passages.

Romans 12

1 Corinthians 12

Ephesians 4

**2. Review your spiritual gift inventory.** You should have completed your inventory since the last session. What is your gift?

**3. Carry-Through Activity — The Service Project.** Continue working on your service project. Spend about an hour depending on the kind of project selected.

**4. Debrief.** Debrief and discuss with your group afterward.

- What you did
- Your feelings about your service

- The commandment of Jesus to love one another.

## Evaluation

How does your gift relate to the service project?

**Get ready for the next session**

Make any arrangements necessary to continue your service project. Conduct inductive Bible study of the following passage before the next session: 1 Peter 4:7-11.

# Maturing in Service

Destination

God plans for members of a church to function as one body. Although the spiritual gifts are many, when used together they allow the church body to minister to the needs of the whole person.

**Lesson Aim:** Each disciple will identify personal gifts, and seek to use them.

---

Disciple**Words**

*Passage: 1 Peter 4:7-11*
*Key Verse: 1 Peter 4:10*

---

**Preparation for the trip checklist:**

○ I have prayed faithfully for myself and my disciple(s) and/or disciple maker.

○ I have read the lesson aim.

○ I have read and studied the Bible passage.

○ I have memorized the key verse.

○ I have completed my personal discipleship assignments and am prepared to evaluate/be evaluated by my fellow disciples.

○ I have made the necessary preparations for the service project for this session.

The following paragraph shows how the gifts work in collective harmony from start to finish. When used together, the gifts fulfill both the *going* and the *teaching* commands of the Great Commission (Matthew 28:18-20). Every church member should cooperate in all elements of the Great Commission, but some may specialize in certain areas because of specific gifts.

Evangelists are gifted to win the lost. Prophets help disciple others by making them aware of sin. Teachers impart doctrine from the Word of God. Exhorters encourage believers to grow in faith. Pastors help shepherd and guide them. Those with the gift of mercy comfort in time of crisis. Servers give a helping hand. Givers extend financial aid and serve as an example in tithing. Administrators provide leadership for their newfound faith. Finally, the entire church provides fellowship.

Review session 6.6. This week you are meeting at the location of your service project or have made plans to go directly after the Bible study portion of this lesson.

According to *Connecting With God,* the gospel had thrived in Asia Minor (modern-day Turkey) for more than a decade, but persecution was ahead for those believers. Peter wrote this letter to prepare them to keep the faith under duress. The theme is suffering for Jesus.

Study 1 Peter 4:7-11 to forge the truths into principles. Pray for God's instruction in finding the principles to apply. Study the passages, answering the three basic inductive Bible study questions.

# Observation

1. Who is the author?

2. Who is involved/addressed?

3. When was the book written? When does it take place?

4. What are the key words? (nouns, verbs)

5. What key words/phrases are repeated?

6. What is being compared? (like, as)

7. What is being contrasted? (but)

8. What are the cause/effect relationships? (therefore, for)

9. What form is used? (parable, narrative, poetry)

# Interpretation

1. How is the passage affected by its biblical/ historical context?

2. How does the passage relate to its immediate context?

3. How does this passage compare with other related passages?

4. What terms or ideas need to be researched?

5. Summarize the passage/paragraph in one sentence (main idea).

## Application

1. Is there a promise to claim or a truth to believe?

2. Is there an example to follow?

3. Is there an attitude to change or a sin to confess?

4. Is there a command to obey?

5. Is there an error to avoid?

6. Is there something to praise God for?

**1. Study the three main passages which list spiritual gifts.** Review your list of the gifts. What do they mean? The following is an alphabetical list of the gifts. Use your Bible and whatever resources you have to look each up. A spiritual gift is the God-given capacity of every Christian to carry out his/her function in the body of Christ.

**Administration.** 1 Corinthians 12:28 — from the Greek word meaning "to steer or guide," this gift is given to assist the church with organization and planning.

**Apostle.** Ephesians 4:11; 1 Corinthians 12:28 — from the Greek word meaning "one who is sent," this gift was given to provide churches with leadership and guidance.

**Discernment.** 1 Corinthians 12:10 — to distinguish spiritual truth from error.

**Evangelism.** Ephesians 4:11 — to spread the good news of the gospel.

**Exhortation.** Romans 12:8 — from the Greek word meaning to come alongside, this gift was given to provide encouragement and counsel.

**Faith.** 1 Corinthians 12:8-10 — to trust God and His promises with a conviction that cannot be shaken.

**Giving.** Romans 12:8 — the ability to share material resources to support the work of the church.

**Healing.** 1 Corinthians 12:9, 28, 30 — to be used by God to help others be made whole either physically, emotionally, mentally, or spiritually.

**Helps.** 1 Corinthians 12:28 — to assist others in the church body in order to enable them to be more effective in their own ministry.

**Knowledge.** 1 Corinthians 12:8 — to learn and gather information from the Bible and other sources of truth.

**Leadership.** Romans 12:8 — to motivate and guide people to accomplish goals of the church body.

**Mercy.** Romans 12:8 — to be sympathetic and empathetic toward those who are suffering.

**Miracles.** 1 Corinthians 12:10, 28 — to be enabled to perform supernatural deeds through God's power.

**Pastor.** Ephesians 4:11 — to spiritually lead, guide, and equip a church body for the work of ministry.

**Prophecy.** Romans 12:6; 1 Corinthians 12:10; Ephesians 4:11 — from the Greek word meaning "to speak forth," this gift includes foretelling and forth telling the message of God.

**Service.** Romans 12:7 — to identify and complete tasks in God's work, however menial.

**Teaching.** Romans 12:7; 1 Corinthians 12:28;

Ephesians 4:11 — to instruct others in God's Word to facilitate growth and maturity.

**Tongues.** 1 Corinthians 12:10; 14:27-28 — the supernatural ability to speak in a language not previously learned so unbelievers can hear the Good News in their own language.

**Interpretation of Tongues.** 1 Corinthians 12:10; 14:27, 28 — to translate the message of someone who has spoken in a language not previously learned.

**Wisdom.** 1 Corinthians 12:8 — to properly apply knowledge and spiritual truths to life and ministry.

**2. Carry-Through Activity — The Service Project.** Conclude the service project. Discuss: Are you currently serving in the area you are gifted? Is there a better place of service that matches your gift? How does your spiritual gift help you serve?

**3. The Great Commission and Serving.** How is your service fulfilling the Great Commission?

**4. Continue service project?** As this series of lessons ends, evaluate and consider whether or not to continue the service project. Make sure your service does not end with this series of lessons; seek and select a new one.

## Evaluation

What is your spiritual gift?

How are you using it?

What more do you know about what Jesus taught?

## Series Evaluation

How do you serve?

How is faith important in serving?

Are you able to teach others how to serve? In other words, are you ready to be a disciple maker in the discipline of service?

### Get ready for the next session

Your next session will begin your final step in the *DiscipleWay* series as you undertake becoming a disciple maker to others. Prepare for the session by doing an inductive study of 1 Samuel 16:1-13. Memorize the key verse for the discipline, 1 Corinthians 11:1. Begin now to identify faithful believers that you will guide through the *DiscipleWay* process.

# Key verse for the discipline

"But so shall it not be among you: but whosoever will be great among you, shall be your minister" (Mark 10:43).

## 6.1 Key Verse

"Thou shalt fear the LORD thy God, and serve him, and shalt swear by his name" (Deuteronomy 6:13).

## 6.2 Key Verse

"Let this mind be in you, which was also in Christ Jesus" (Philippians 2:5).

## 6.3 Key Verse

"I am the vine, ye are the branches: He that abideth in me, and I in him, the same bringeth forth much fruit: for without me ye can do nothing" (John 15:5).

## 6.4 Key Verse

"As the Father hath loved me, so have I loved you: continue ye in my love" (John 15:9).

## 6.5 Key Verse

"If ye were of the world, the world would love his own: but because ye are not of the world, but I have chosen you out of the world, therefore the world hateth you" (John 15:19).

## 6.6 Key Verse

"For I say, through the grace given unto me, to every man that is among you, not to think of himself more highly than he ought to think; but to think soberly, according as God hath dealt to every man the measure of faith" (Romans 12:3).

## 6.7 Key Verse

"As every man hath received the gift, even so minister the same one to another, as good stewards of the manifold grace of God" (1 Peter 4:10).

www.ingramcontent.com/pod-product-compliance
Lightning Source LLC
Chambersburg PA
CBHW081242020426
42331CB00013B/3268